Introduction

This book was written to answer some of the more common questions associated with takings by a governmental entity, generally known as eminent domain or condemnation. It should be used as a guide to understanding common issues and problems associated with takings, so you are better prepared to speak with your legal counsel about your case and you are in a better position to understand and weigh the risks and benefits associated with an eminent domain taking.

Although this book was written to help a property owner, business owner or tenant understand the eminent domain process, it is not meant as a substitute for hiring good legal counsel. This is critically important in cases involving property rights, such as eminent domain. Eminent domain can be very complicated and involves knowledge of several areas of law such as land use, administrative law, governmental law, zoning law, and environmental law, to name a few.

Given that all attorney's fees and costs are paid by the condemning authority, there should never be an excuse for a property owner, business owner, or tenant to attempt to navigate the intricacies of eminent domain by themselves. Use of a good eminent domain attorney will ensure that the value the condemning authority is offering for your property, and any damages caused by the taking, are being paid in full.

So many times property owners, business owners or tenants have settled their claims with a condemning authority without the advice of a good eminent domain attorney, only to find out that they were paid far below market value for their property, or that their remaining property is now worth far less after the taking. A good eminent domain attorney, with at least 10 years of experience, will examine the taking and will hire the experts needed to properly evaluate the case. The condemning authority must pay all of the attorney's fees and costs for the property owner, business owner or tenant. Therefore, there is no excuse for not hiring eminent domain counsel and the experts necessary to determine if you are being paid fair market value and full compensation for the taking of your property rights.

About the Author

Mr. Bruschi is a Board Certified Attorney practicing eminent domain and real estate law throughout the State of Florida. He focuses his practice on eminent domain litigation, commercial litigation and general real property litigation. Mr. Bruschi also conducts numerous real estate closings and is a certified title agent in the State of Florida. A former Assistant State Attorney and Assistant County Attorney for Broward County, Mr. Bruschi also has experience in land use and administrative law matters.

Mr. Bruschi is Board Certified by The Florida Bar as a specialist in City, County, and Local Government Law and is past Chair of the Bar's Certification Committee. He is AV rated by Martindale-Hubbell, a significant rating accomplishment for attorneys - a testament to the fact that a lawyer's peers rank him or her at the highest level of professional excellence.

Mr. Bruschi is an adjunct professor of law at Nova Southeastern Shepard Broad Law Center. As an adjunct law professor, Mr. Bruschi has taught eminent domain and real property law for over 10 years.

Mr. Bruschi has been published numerous times. His article "The Survey of Florida Evidence," was published in the Nova Law Review from 1991-1996. Mr. Bruschi also published an article in the American Bar Journal, Local Government Section entitled, "Researching on the Internet." While in law school, Mr. Bruschi served as Editor-in-Chief of the Nova Law Review and authored an article entitled, "The Establishment Clause & the Supreme Court," 10 Nova L. Rev. 275 (1986).

Mr. Bruschi's eminent domain practice is statewide, from the Florida Keys to Pensacola Florida, and he is often found working throughout the State of Florida on his cases. Mr. Bruschi is a licensed pilot with an instrument rating and uses his small plane to travel throughout the state for his eminent domain practice and real estate practice.

Mr. Bruschi earned his law degree, magna cum laude, at Nova Southeastern University, Shepard Broad Law Center, in 1987, and earned his bachelor of science degree at the University of Florida, in 1978. He was admitted to The Florida Bar in 1987 and is admitted to practice before the United States Supreme Court, the 11th Circuit Court of Appeals, the Federal District Court, Southern District of Florida, and all courts in the state of Florida.

Mr. Bruschi is a member of The Florida Bar and The Florida Bar's Eminent Domain Committee. He is also a member of the American Bar Association, the Broward County Bar Association, the Federal Bar Association, and the Federal Trial Bar.

A PROPERTY, TENANT AND BUSINESS OWNER'S GUIDE TO EMINENT DOMAIN IN FLORIDA©

Dale A. Bruschi, Esq.

Table of Contents

What is Eminent Domain?

Eminent domain is the fundamental power of the sovereign to take private property for a public use without the owner's consent. The sovereign means the state or federal government. Most eminent domain in Florida is carried out by the State of Florida, or by one of its agencies such as the Florida Department of Transportation (FDOT) or a political subdivision such as a city or county. The state is allowed to delegate its eminent domain power to many different agencies and political subdivisions throughout Florida.

The power of eminent domain is an inherent attribute of sovereignty that is not derived from the Constitution and is absolute, except as limited by the Constitution. Eminent domain is unique and is quite different than all other federal and state laws. Unlike the Constitution and statutes that grants the government its power, yet limits it at the same time, the inherent power of eminent domain does not arise from either the Constitution or the statutes. It is inherent in being the sovereign or supreme authority. Like the kings (i.e., the sovereigns) of old, all land was owned by the king, who would grant title. From the beginning, the sovereign owned all land and that holds true today for the state, which as the sovereign, owns all land. The power of eminent domain is implied from the "superior dominion" – the eminent domain – which the state holds over all the soil within its bounds, and to which the right of an individual to own and acquire property is subject.

The power of eminent domain arises from the practical necessity to take properties for the public good. Every property owner who holds title to property is subject to the superior right of the government to retake that property. This power to retake property is only limited by the State and Federal Constitutions. The Federal Constitution requires "just compensation" (the Fifth Amendment), but the Constitution for the state of Florida (Article X, section 6) has a higher standard and requires "full compensation." Additionally, the State and Federal Constitutions require a public purpose or public use. The requirement to pay compensation for property taken by the government and the requirement that the property taken must be for a public purpose or use are limitations on the government's exercise of its eminent domain power.

The terms *eminent domain* and *condemnation* refer to the intentional takings by government through the condemnation process. The terms are used interchangeably and mean the same thing when the government takes your property.

Why is Eminent Domain Used?

In order to build public schools, libraries, roads, parks, water lines, drainage, sewage lines, electrical lines, hospitals, and hundreds of other public buildings and projects, the government, federal, state, and its local agencies and political subdivisions must acquire property. If title to property were absolute, in other words, if no one could take title from the owner, then civilization as we know it would grind to a halt. If property could not be acquired, no roads would be built; there would be no parks; there would be no sewage and drainage lines; and there would be no electrical lines. All of these items, and hundreds like them, serve a public purpose, but oftentimes the land must be acquired through the forced taking of property known as eminent domain.

In fact, many nations outside of the United States utilize a form of eminent domain to forcefully acquire property. The main difference between the use of eminent domain in the United States and the use of eminent domain in a foreign country is our Constitution. Our Federal and State Constitutions have two requirements that many foreign countries do not and that is: (1) The acquisition of property must be for a public purpose or public use, and (2) The property owner must be paid "just" or "full" compensation if their property is taken. In many foreign countries property can be confiscated by the government and owners are not paid for the property when the government takes it.

Additionally, a government in a foreign country can take property for any reason, even to give to another private person. In the United States the power to take property is limited, and the taking of property must be for a public purpose. Property cannot be taken by the government and given to a private party for their personal use and enjoyment, because this is not a public purpose or a public use.

Who can use Eminent Domain in Florida?

The exercise of the power of eminent domain and the constitutional limitations on that power are vested in the legislature. The right to exercise the power of eminent domain can be delegated by the legislature to the agencies of government and implemented by legislative enactment. This means that the state government can pass a law and delegate the power of eminent domain to an agent or political subdivision of the state. This agent is also referred to as the condemnor. In fact, the only way any entity can wield the power of eminent domain is if a specific law has delegated them the power to do so. Interestingly, the legislature can delegate the power of eminent domain, but can also restrict the extent of the eminent domain power to the particular entity it is delegating the power. In other words, they can restrict the eminent domain power to a school for "school purposes only." Therefore, a school delegated the power of eminent domain could not go out and start to condemn property to build roads, unless the school could prove a school purpose.

Currently, there are hundreds of entities that have been delegated the eminent domain power in the State of Florida. The biggest condemnors in the state have generally been the FDOT, counties, and then cities.

Here is a list of some of the wide-ranging entities that can utilize the power of eminent domain to acquire property:

- Airports
- Armory Board
- Beach and Shore Preservation Authorities
- Community College District Boards of Trustees
- County Hospitals
- Department of Children and Families
- Department of Corrections
- Department of Health
- Division of Bond Finance
- Division of Forestry
- Division of Parks and Recreation
- Drainage Districts
- Expressway Authority
- Florida Recreational Trails System

- Mosquito Control Districts
- Port Facility Operators
- Public Housing Authorities
- Railroad and Canal Companies
- Regional Transportation Authorities
- Rural Electric Cooperatives
- School Boards
- Special Fire Control Districts
- State Colleges
- Telephone and Telegraph Companies
- Tri-County Rail Authority
- University Board of Trustees
- Water and Sewer Companies
- Water Management Districts

What is a Public Purpose?

The Florida Constitution (Article X, section 6), expressly prohibits the use of the power of eminent domain "except for a public purpose." The terms public purpose and public use are oftentimes used interchangeably in eminent domain. A public purpose is a taking of property that will benefit the public, or the property will be used by the public. If the taking of the property solely benefits a private person or private entity, then the public purpose limitation on the government's power has been violated.

Oftentimes, a public project will have an incidental private benefit. In other words, the acquisition of property for a public parking garage may benefit private businesses that are near the parking garage. As long as the public purpose or public use predominates the incidental private benefit, the acquisition will be upheld and the public purpose sustained by the courts.

Before an entity with the power of eminent domain can take your property, they must prove to the court that the property will be used for a public purpose. Roads are a good example of public purpose as the public in general will use the roadway system to move about. However, private businesses and private homeowners will also benefit from the use of the road system, but again, this is considered incidental to the main use by the public in general.

Why is it Necessary for the Government to Condemn my Property?

When the government, or any agency with the power of eminent domain (the condemnor), comes to condemn your property, they must first prove they have a public purpose for your property. However, they must also prove that your particular land is necessary for their public purpose. Public necessity is essential to the valid exercise of the power of eminent domain. The condemning authority must present to the court a reasonable, not absolute, necessity for your property. Sometimes a condemning authority tries to acquire more land than is needed for its public project. In these instances, the condemning authority may have a public purpose, but cannot demonstrate to the court why it is necessary to have as much land as they are trying to condemn.

As an example, if the condemning authority is attempting to widen a road from two lanes to four lanes, its engineers would design the road for four lanes. The engineers then determine how much more right of way will be needed along the road so that a four-lane road with medians and shoulders can be built. They determine that to build this four-lane road they will need to take 50 feet from each side of the present two-lane road. However, in this instance, when the government files its condemnation to take the land for the road they decide to take 75 feet on each side of the road; although, to build its road it is only necessary for the condemning authority to have 50 feet. Therefore, their taking of the additional 25 feet is simply not necessary to accomplish their public purpose.

The condemning authority oftentimes tries to come into court to explain that they need the additional 25 feet in case they decide to expand the road in the future to six lanes. However, the need must be reasonable, and if the condemning authority has no reasonable plans to expand the road in the near future, the taking of the additional land will be deemed to be unnecessary and not reasonable for their present project. The courts should disallow the acquisition of the additional area because it is not necessary for their present project.

What is Full Compensation?

In Florida, when the condemning authority takes property, it must attempt to make the property owner whole again, as if the property were never taken. **When all of the property owner's property is acquired, then full compensation would be the fair market value of the property at its highest and best use.** Highest and best use of the property may be for something other than for what the property is presently being used. This is where the value of the property taken in condemnation can vary from the average property sale.

Let me give an example to illustrate this concept. A person has a piece of property along a waterway. He is presently using the property as his personal home. Although the property is his home, the local land use codes would allow a high-rise building to be constructed on the site. Therefore, the highest and best use of the property is not for a family home (which may have a lower value), but is for a high-rise apartment building. Consequently, the property owner should be paid for the property at its highest and best use as a high-rise site and not as a personal home.

Ultimately, the goal of full compensation is to try to put the property owner in as good a position as possible, as though the taking had never occurred. Oftentimes, this is done by compensating the property owner for the loss of his or her property. Other times, if it is a partial taking, it will require returning the remaining property, as close as possible, to the form it was in before the taking. In other words, if you had two entrances before the taking, then after the taking you would still want to have two entrances. If you could not have two entrances because it is no longer physically possible, then the government must attempt to provide the necessary compensation to attempt to make the property owner whole. This is the idea behind full compensation.

What is Fair Market Value?

In eminent domain, fair market value has been the accepted starting point to determine full compensation in the State of Florida. The courts in Florida have generally adhered to the fair market value standard, but have stated that it is not the only element for full compensation in the state. The theory and purpose of the constitutional guarantee of full compensation is that the owner will be made whole, as far as possible and practicable.

The Florida courts have defined fair market value as the amount of money that a purchaser willing, but not obliged to buy the property, would pay an owner willing, but not obliged to sell, taking into consideration all uses to which the property is adapted and might be applied. In Florida, this is known as the willing buyer-willing seller test of market value. The key to understanding fair market value in Florida is that it takes into consideration uses other than for what the property is currently being used.

As an illustration, a property owner owns a piece of property on a corner of a busy intersection on which his single-family home sits. The current use of the property is for single-family residential. If the property were to be condemned to widen the road, the fair market value would include a consideration of many factors affecting valuation.

The following are but some of the factors that a willing buyer and a willing seller would probably consider in their negotiations in determining the fair market value of a piece of property, and which an experienced eminent domain attorney and his experts can point out and help develop during the case:

- Size and shape of the land
- Elevation of the land
- Relationship to streets, thoroughfares, and utilities
- Location and connection with trends of growth of the area
- Changing trends in the neighborhood
- Zoning and building restrictions
- Recent sales price of the land
- Recent sales prices of similar or comparable properties
- Uses to which the property is adaptable
- Preliminary development plans and improvements to the property

If the single-family home on the corner of a busy intersection were better suited for a commercial use, such as a gas station or convenience store, then the fair market value of the property would be what a willing buyer and seller would pay for the property, after taking into consideration all uses for which the property could be legally adapted.

What is Highest and Best Use?

One of the first things I learned in eminent domain was to view property not as it is today, but as it could be one day in its highest and best use. Highest and best use is a key concept in eminent domain and one that is needed to provide the property owner with full compensation for the taking of his or her property or property rights. **The valuation of condemned land does not depend on the current nor the anticipated use of the property; the value is to be determined from a consideration of all available uses.** In the language of appraisers, this is known as the "highest and best use." **Highest and best use has been defined as "the highest and most profitable use for which the property is adaptable and needed, or is likely to be needed in the near future."**

In Florida, two separate factors are included in determining the highest and best use of property. First, the property must be adaptable or suitable for the use. Second, there must be a demand for the use currently or in the near future. If someone wanted to argue that property being used for agricultural has a highest and best use of industrial use, evidence would have to be presented that the property was adaptable or suitable for this use and that there is a demand for industrial property now or in the near future.

An experienced eminent domain attorney working with appraisers and land planners can help determine if a piece of property that is being condemned is being utilized in its highest and best use. If the property is not being utilized for its highest and best use the experienced attorney can get a determination from his experts if the property is adaptable or suitable for another use, and if there is a demand for this use. Consequently, hiring experienced eminent domain counsel can help you determine the highest and best use of the property, and maximize the fair market value of the property.

What if the Government Takes my Property and Doesn't pay for it?

In an eminent domain action, the government essentially sues you to give you money for the property it is taking from you. The government takes away your property through a forced taking, and through court process. This court proceeding is one of the only actions of its kind where the government actually sues you to give you money. The government may need your property to widen its road and, before it widens the road, it will acquire the property it needs from you through eminent domain.

But what if the government builds its road on your property, without your consent, and does not pay you for the property it is using, or taking from you? When this happens the property owner must sue the government to recover the compensation for the property the government has acquired. Inverse condemnation is the cause of action the property or landowner would file against the government to recover compensation for a taking of property when condemnation proceedings have not been instituted. Therefore, when the government files suit to take your property and pay you compensation for the taking, this is eminent domain. When the government takes your property without filing suit against you and paying you compensation for the property it has taken, and the property owner must file suit against the government to recover compensation for the property that has been taken, this is known as inverse condemnation.

How Does Eminent Domain Begin?

Years before the condemning authority comes to take your property or business, a process has been in place to determine the need for your property. Each condemning authority's process to determine the need for private property is a little bit different, but I will describe a general procedure for how the eminent domain process begins.

For example, in a typical roadway project, a condemning authority will conduct studies years in advance to determine the need to widen the road. First, they will take traffic counts to determine the amount of traffic on the roadway, and the times of the year that the traffic is greatest. They will also determine the increase in traffic on the roadway from year-to-year traffic counts, as well as from a determination of new residential and commercial developments that are in place and are planned for the future. From all this data the condemning authority will project when the level of service on the roadway will start to fail. In other words, the condemning authority will determine when the roadway will no longer allow the smooth flow of traffic, when it will start to cause traffic jams, and when it will become unsafe.

The projections for when the roadway will fail will be studied by professional engineers and consultants, who will devise a timetable for when the roadway will have to be widened to continue to accommodate traffic at higher volumes. Consequently, they must consider that the property needed to accommodate the widening of the roadway must be acquired prior to when the construction on the roadway will start, and prior to the time the roadway will begin to fail. These procedures are accomplished by conducting long-range planning studies, and placing the project in a 5, 10, 15, or 20-year work program.

Before a roadway project reaches the 5-year work program, a schedule is drafted by the condemning authority. This schedule will include items that must be accomplished over the course of years prior to the acquisition of the property and the construction of the roadway. For instance, in a roadway project some of the first items that must be accomplished will be studies to determine if there are alternative routes; the costs for the various alternative routes; if the roadway will be safe; if there any environmental impacts from this project, and if long range planning studies were conducted. The outcome of these initial studies will determine if the project can meet state and federal standards, and whether the property can be acquired and the roadway constructed. Then, dates will be set to assign a project manager as well as to schedule for right-of-way maps to be completed, and to schedule the completion of the construction plans. Dates will also be set for reviews of the plans; to assign an appraiser to value the parcels for the project; for negotiation of the parcels, to commence and complete condemnation of all needed parcels; and finally, to bid and construct the project.

All during this long process, the condemning authority must make the schedule of their project known to the public. The condemning authority does this by publishing, either in its local offices, or online on its website, the time and places for the various meetings as the project moves forward. In the case of the FDOT (and other condemning authorities), public input on the project is requested. Public workshops are set up through all the stages of the project, and the public has an opportunity to comment on the condemning authority's project, and the impact it will have, both positive and negative, on the property and their lives. Public input on projects can sometimes change the direction, size, location, or scope of the public project. If you are concerned about a public project and its effect on your property, you should contact the agency in charge of the project, and they can direct you to all the information you will need to understand what is happening with the project and when it will happen.

Will the Government Negotiate Before Suit is Filed?

Yes, the government (a/k/a the condemning authority) is required to negotiate with you before an eminent domain lawsuit is filed. Under the current Florida Statures, section 73.015, before the government can file an eminent domain suit against your property, it must attempt to negotiate in good faith with the property owner and must provide the property owner with a w r i t t e n offer. This written offer must be based upon a valid appraisal. Generally, the acquisition agent for the condemning authority will come to your door and attempt to discuss an acquisition price for the property. As anything you say to the acquisition agent can later be used against you in court, we recommend that you have your attorney speak with the acquisition agent.

There are a couple of things to remember when negotiating with the condemning authority. First, the condemning authority will attempt to acquire the property at the lowest price possible. There is nothing wrong with this, but you must realize that even though they have an appraisal done on the property, there is no guarantee that their appraiser has considered the highest comparable sales available, or that the government's appraiser has considered the severance damages to the remaining property. Second, there are many intricacies when valuing property in eminent domain. Eminent domain appraisals are entirely different from bank appraisals. The most important difference is the fact that on many parcels there are severance, or the damages that the taking has done to the remaining property. Oftentimes, the severance, or remainder, damages are more important than the value of the property that has actually been acquired. The reason for this is that the taking can render your remaining property useless. Yet, you will still be required to pay taxes on it, and you can still be sued if someone is injured on your remaining property. Additionally, when the size of your property changes, your remaining property, and any improvements on the remaining property, may not conform to the local codes and ordinances. This could require you to come out of pocket for enormous expenses, should the property be required to be brought back up to code.

People tend to assume that because the condemning authority has an appraisal, that it must be correct. Please keep in mind that appraisals are subjective. In other words, two appraisers will often differ as to comparable sales properties, severance damages, and a host of other factors that affect valuation. A property owner's appraised value can differ significantly from a condemning authority's appraised value. This is because certain determinations and assumptions that must be made in an appraisal can greatly affect its final value. Additionally, other experts may be needed to review and interpret the local codes and ordinances. Engineers might be needed to review traffic and traffic circulation on the property, or review drainage issues for the property. Land planners might be needed to determine the effect of the local jurisdiction's codes and ordinances on the property, and how the taking will affect the remainder. A general contractor might be needed to determine the cost of replacing or repairing improvements on the property. A landscape architect may be needed to determine the cost of the landscaping and how much will be needed to be replaced on the remainder to keep it in compliance with the code.

In an eminent domain matter, all the experts needed to review the condemning authority's appraisal and to develop your own appraised value are free to you. Under the eminent domain statutes, the condemning authority is responsible for paying all fees and costs so that you can make your own independent determination of the value for the property that was taken, and any property you have remaining. The payment of fees and costs are there to protect the property owner's interests when his or her land is being taken by the government. Once you agree to a price with the condemning authority and you sign all the paperwork, you cannot later go back and claim more compensation, even if you have made a mistake. It is recommended that you exercise your right to hire an eminent domain attorney and your own independent experts, so that a proper determination of full compensation can be made on your property and you are fully compensated.

Will the Government Negotiate After Suit is Filed?

Yes, the government will continue to negotiate with you after suit is filed. When an eminent domain case is filed, the trial court requires both parties to a lawsuit to go to mediation to attempt to resolve the matter, prior to a jury trial. This saves the trial court precious judicial resources and allows the parties to have certainty in the amount that will be needed to settle the matter. Additionally, a mediation saves an enormous amount of time as a trial and an appeal can take months or years in the court system.

Sometimes, a mediation of the matter is good for other reasons. Generally, in an eminent domain trial the only issue is one of compensation. In other words, the trial is just about dollars and cents. However, in a mediation the opportunity to work out other nonmonetary compensation is possible. For instance, if you are a property owner and a median is going in the new road, you might be able to negotiate with the condemning authority to put in a median opening so that cars from both directions will have access to your property. Oftentimes, this can be more valuable than just the monetary compensation. It can only be obtained in negotiations and cannot be obtained in a trial of the matter.

How can the Government Acquire my Property Before full Payment?

In eminent domain, certain condemning authorities, for certain types of projects, can acquire property prior to final judgment. This is known as a *quick taking*. Quick taking allows a condemning authority to acquire the needed property and begin its project prior to a final judgment and payment of any remaining compensation.

Chapter 74 of the Florida Statutes allows certain named condemning authorities, such as the FDOT, the county or a municipality, to acquire property in advance of final judgment by filing a Declaration of Taking, along with its eminent domain petition. The Declaration of Taking must contain the description of the property to be taken by the condemning authority and a good faith estimate of value, based upon a valid appraisal for the property that is going to be taken.

In order to acquire the property prior to the final judgment, the condemning authority must call up a hearing before the trial judge to put forth its evidence as to why it should be allowed to acquire the property in advance of final judgment. **This is known as an Order of Taking hearing.** An Order of Taking is a mini trial without a jury. The condemning authority can take the property if it can prove to the judge at this hearing that the authority has the following: a public purpose, a public necessity, a good faith estimate of value, and it has met all the statutory conditions precedent to bringing a suit in eminent domain. If the condemning authority can prove this in the hearing, then the burden shifts to the property owner to prove that the condemning authority acted in bad faith or abused its discretion. The court determines whether to grant the Order of Taking by determining whether competent and substantial evidence has been presented to support acquiring the property in advance of final judgment.

How Does an Eminent Domain Trial Work?

An eminent domain trial works exactly as any other civil trial, except with one important difference. In an eminent domain trial you will have 12 jurors, not 6 jurors as in other civil trials. A judge will give the parties a pretrial order to comply with discovery (discovery is simply the legal procedure to discover information about the other side's case), and to attempt to mediate the case. The judge will also give the parties a trial date along with a pretrial conference. At the pretrial conference, the judge will ask both parties if they are ready for trial, and if they are, he or she will ask how many days they will need for the trial. Generally, there are numerous cases that are ready for trial at the same time. However, by statute, the eminent domain trial is to be taken first by the judge. This does not always happen due to scheduling conflicts, but it is one of the only areas of the law that has preference at trial over other civil matters. An eminent domain trial, from start to finish, averages about five business days. Some trials are shorter and some can be considerably longer, going weeks at a time.

Once a trial date is chosen and the amount of time is determined, both parties will arrive in court for the first day of trial. The judge will ask if there are any preliminary matters to resolve such as pretrial motions. After the court resolves any pretrial matters, a jury pool is brought into the courtroom. Because eminent domain trials have 12 jurors, instead of six, a larger panel will be brought into the courtroom for selection. The judge will place 12 jurors in the panel, and the questioning of the jurors will begin -- first by the condemning authority's attorney, and then by the property owner's attorney.

Once 12 jurors and two alternates are selected, the judge will ask each attorney if they want to make an opening statement. The condemning authority's attorney gets to go first, followed by the property owner's attorney. Each will outline his or her case and what evidence he or she will present to the jury. Once the opening statements have concluded, the condemning authority will get to call its first witness. The condemning authority will generally call all the preliminary expert witnesses needed to support the opinion of its appraiser. Generally, the last witness the condemning authority will call will be its appraiser to give his or her opinion on fair market value for the property. The property owner's attorney gets to cross-examine each of the condemning authority's witnesses to point out weaknesses in the condemning authority's case.

Once the condemning authority has rested its case, the judge will ask the parties if they have any motions to be made at the close of this stage of the case. After hearing any motions, the judge will then allow the property owner's attorney to present his or her expert witnesses, which the condemning authority will then be able to cross-examine. After the close of all the evidence, the judge will entertain any motions as it pertains to the trial to this point. After those motions are heard and determined, the judge will then have a charging conference to hear the jury instructions that each party would like to have read to the jury. At some point during the trial, the jury will be taken to view the property that has been taken. This is known as the jury view, and it is unique to eminent domain cases. The judge will determine at what part of the case the jury is to view the property. Jury views generally occur at the end of the trial, after both sides have presented their evidence.

Once the charging conference is completed, the judge will call the jury back into the courtroom and both sides will have an opportunity to present their closing arguments -- first, the condemning authority, then the property owner's attorney, and then a rebuttal by the condemning authority. The closing arguments will differ from the opening statements because the attorneys will get to argue to the jury how the evidence presented, and the law that will be read by the trial judge (the jury instructions), should be applied in the case. In other words, each attorney will argue how the facts and the law favors their expert's value for the property.

After the closing arguments are completed, the judge will read the jury instructions (the law in the case) and will send the jurors back to deliberate. The jurors must come to a unanimous decision as to the issues in the case, which include the amount of full compensation to be awarded to the property owner. The alternate jurors will not deliberate and will then be released by the trial judge, provided there are 12 jurors to deliberate the matter.

Once the jury makes a determination in the case, the judge is notified and everyone is brought back into the courtroom. The judge will then read the jury's verdict to everyone in the courtroom. After the verdict is read, the judge will thank the jurors for their service and release them from jury duty.

Can I Appeal the Government's Taking of my Property or Business?

Yes, you can appeal the government's taking of your property or business, if there are adequate grounds. This is generally done in a quick taking proceeding, if the judge enters the Order of Taking for the condemning authority. An appeal must be made within 30 days after the judge enters the order. However, this does not automatically stay the taking of the property by the condemning authority. A separate stay order must be entered by the trial court to stop the condemning authority from going onto the acquired property and beginning its project.

If the Order of Taking is not appealed and there were adequate grounds for an appeal, then the acquisition of the property by the condemning authority generally cannot later be challenged, absent extraordinary circumstances such as fraud. At the end of the trial, if the amount of compensation is not adequate and there are sufficient grounds, an appeal can be made after the final judgment on the jury verdict has been entered by the trial court. This must be done within 30 days of the trial judge rendering the final judgment.

If the eminent domain matter is filed as a slow taking, meaning that possession of the property and full compensation will all be decided at the time of trial, then, if there are sufficient grounds, an appeal can be made on both the issue of possession and the issue of full compensation at the end of the jury trial.

How Does Eminent Domain Affect my Property?

Eminent domain can have a dramatic effect on your property. If you have a full taking of your property, there are fewer issues and it will be just a matter of getting an appropriate value for the acquisition of your entire parcel of land and any improvements. **However, the most important and dramatic effect on your property will be if there is a partial taking and you have property remaining after the government's taking.**

The reason for this dramatic effect is because on each parcel of property there are certain statutes, codes and ordinances that govern the use and development of any piece of property. When a condemning authority takes a piece of that property and that taking changes the size, shape and quantity of the remaining property, it can leave the remaining property in violations of those laws and, consequently, severely damaged. I will illustrate this with a simple example.

Let's assume that you purchased one acre of property and you paid $100,000 for that property. The statutes, codes and ordinances state that you need one acre of property to build a single-family home. The government comes along and needs 10 percent of your property to widen its road. They make you an offer and they say, since you just paid $100,000, and they are acquiring only 10 percent, then full compensation for the property they are acquiring is $10,000. If you were to accept this amount, you could be devastated.

Why? The reason is simple. If you no longer have one acre of property as required by the codes, then you cannot build a single family home. What can you do with your remaining property? If this was the only improvement that could be built on the 1-acre property, then the value of your remaining property is zero. You have now lost $90,000 of the $100,000 you paid for the property. This is known as severance or remainder damages.

Had you hired an eminent domain attorney, and he or she hired the necessary experts, they would have discovered that your damages would have been $100,000, or more. Why? Because if you cannot develop the property, the damages are the amount you paid for the property, plus any taxes or assessments you will still owe on the property, plus the liability you will still have on the property should someone be injured on the property. To make you whole and pay you full compensation, the government would, at the very least, have to pay you for the value of the entire property or $100,000.

This is a simple example, but there are many more complex issues in eminent domain when property is taken. Without an experienced attorney with experts to review the condemnor's taking, your property and improvements could be rendered worthless. If you did not properly have your case investigated by eminent domain professionals, you could be left with a worthless piece of property, and you could still be liable for taxes or injuries that occur on your remaining property.

The eminent domain laws were set up so that property owners would be on an even playing field with large governmental organizations with millions of dollars to spend on their eminent domain projects. The constitutional mandate of full compensation requires that the government pay for your attorney's fees and expert fees so that a proper determination can be made as to the full compensation the government owes you.

How Does Eminent Domain Affect my Business?

Eminent domain can have a dramatic effect on your business. If there is a <u>full taking</u> of the property and the business resides within the area of the acquisition, then no business damages are paid by the government. When there is a full taking of the business, the business is only eligible for trade fixtures they have placed on the property, and if there is time on the lease and the lease does not specifically exclude it, then the business owner may be eligible for a leasehold interest.

If there is a partial taking of property, the business is eligible for business damages. The business could also be severely damaged or completely shut down by the taking. The statutes, codes and ordinances that govern the use and development of the property will also come into play when there is a business on the property. Those laws designate how much parking a business will need, designate the setbacks from the roadway or other government improvements, and will also designate how much landscape and buffering is needed on a property.

In a partial taking, the acquisition of land by the condemning authority will affect all the codes for the property and improvements that remain. Generally, there are provisions in the codes to allow an improvement or business to continue even if it becomes nonconforming due to a condemnation. The problem with this is that the local jurisdictions will not allow a nonconformity to be enlarged, or sometimes continued past a certain period of time. If the building on your property is nonconforming, and, for example, a hurricane damaged the building, there is a strong possibility that the entire building would need to be brought up to code when it is repaired. If there was nonconforming parking, landscaping or setbacks, you would need to comply with the current code when repairing the building. Sometimes, this will mean that the building can no longer be used for the business, or that a portion of the building will have to be removed so that the building can be brought up to the current code.

The loss of part or all of the building in which the business is housed can be devastating to the business owner. This is why it is necessary to get an eminent domain attorney to investigate and determine how the government's taking will affect the business. In this way, the business owner can be compensated for the loss in business he or she will incur because of the taking, or the business owner can be relocated before the taking occurs so that the business can continue unfettered by the government's taking.

Dale A. Bruschi, Esq.

An experienced eminent domain attorney can properly advise the business owner and can guide him or her through the myriad amount of rules and regulations that govern the eminent domain acquisition, and ensure that the business owner is properly compensated should he or she lose any part of their business. It is advisable to hire an experienced eminent domain attorney as early as possible in the eminent domain matter, since a claim for business damages generally begins long before the actual eminent domain suit is filed. The business damage claim is waived, if not brought within specified time periods. Oftentimes, it may be too late to file a business damage claim if the business owner waits for the eminent domain suit to be filed.

How Does Eminent Domain Affect me if I am a Tenant?

If you are a tenant on a piece of property that is subject to an eminent domain action, you are treated as an owner in the constitutional sense. In other words, you have many of the same rights as the property owner. If you are a tenant running a business on a piece of property being taken by the government, you can be paid for business damages caused by the damage a partial acquisition of the property does to your business. You can also be paid for any trade fixtures you may have placed on the property to run your business. You can also be paid for your leasehold interest. The leasehold interest is the difference between actual rent and the current rate in the market for rent. I will illustrate a leasehold interest in the following example.

You rent a piece of property and your lease term indicates that you must pay $1,000 per month to the landlord or property owner. The lease is for five years with one, five-year option to renew. The lease gives you the right to sublease the property. You can lease the property for your term, and if you are in compliance with your lease, you can exercise the option to renew and continue to sublease the property for an additional term. You lease the property to a subtenant for $2,000 per month. You pay the landlord or property owner $1,000 per month (the actual rent) and you keep the other $1,000 you get from the subtenant (the market rent). As a tenant with a valid lease, you are the owner in the constitutional sense because you have the right to utilize all the rights of the property because of your lease. Because you have the right to lease the property to a subtenant, you have the right to keep any rent amount over that which is called for by your lease. In an eminent domain action, the difference between actual and market rent is paid to the tenant, not the property owner.

The terms of the lease oftentimes spell out the rights and obligations between a tenant and a landlord. If the terms of the lease are silent as to the leasehold interest, the law in Florida allows for a leasehold interest. If the lease specifically excludes a leasehold interest, then in the condemnation action, the tenant may not be allowed to claim a leasehold interest in the property. An experienced eminent domain attorney can help advise the tenant as to his options when a condemnation occurs on the property.

It is advisable to hire an eminent domain attorney at the earliest possible moment as the business damage claims begin to run long before the eminent domain suit is filed. If the tenant waits for the lawsuit to be filed, any business damage claim may be waived.

Why are Experts Used in Eminent Domain?

Many people ask, why use experts in an eminent domain case? The answer is simple, an eminent domain matter can be very complex and an expert opinion is needed to help the jury understand the issues. An opinion of worth generally must come from a person who has the training and background, to give an opinion as to the value of the property in a court of law. These people are known as expert witnesses.

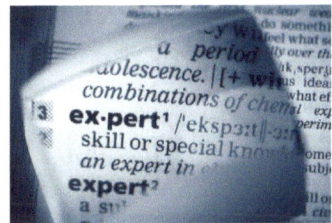

In a condemnation matter, you can have as few as one expert witness, or more than a dozen expert witnesses. Each expert opinion in an eminent domain case helps resolve issues that ultimately impact the fair market value of the property, and any severance or remainder damages to the property when there is a partial taking. In other words, each expert's opinion is helping to resolve a sub-issue that the appraiser must have resolved to form his or her opinion of the fair market value of the property.

Here are some of the experts that are used in an eminent domain trial, and what their purpose is in the case:
- *Appraiser* – The key witness in the case. He or she will look at comparable properties, sales of properties, the income generated by the property, and will give an opinion as to the fair market value of the property and any remainder or severance damages.
- *Land Planner* – He or she will examine the codes and ordinances that affect the property, and will give an expert opinion as to the impact those codes and ordinances will have on the property. The appraiser will use the land planner's opinion in forming his or her expert opinion on the value of the property.

- *Engineer* (civil, traffic, drainage) – The engineers will examine various issues such as traffic, drainage and determine how the taking will impact the property and its remainder. If a cure to the property is needed (such as cutting and refacing a building or replacing parking), the engineer will draft the design for this work and, with the help of a contractor, determine the costs for this work. The appraiser will use this opinion in forming his or her expert opinion on the value of the property.
- *Landscape Architect* – This expert will examine the property in both the before and after condition to determine if the property will still meet the code for landscaping requirements for the property. As with the other experts, the appraiser will use this expert opinion in forming his or her opinion of value.
- *General Contractor* – If any work is needed on the property, a general contractor will determine the costs for permitting and the costs for doing the work on the site. The appraiser will use this opinion in forming his or her expert opinion of value.
- *Fixture Appraiser* – If fixtures or trade fixtures associated with the property are taken or damaged, then a trade fixture expert will give an opinion as to the fair market value of the trade fixtures. The appraiser will utilize this opinion in forming his or her opinion of the fair market value of the property.
- *Marketing Analyst* – Sometimes, the market analyst is utilized when it is difficult to make a good determination on the demand for a particular type of real estate product in the marketplace.
- *Forensic Accountant* – This expert is utilized to determine the value of a business and will render an expert opinion as to the value of the business if the business is a total loss, or will render an expert opinion as to the damages to the business if the business is not a total loss.

The utilization of expert witnesses familiar with the eminent domain statutes and case law is very important. Certain elements of an eminent domain case require that the experts be familiar with the eminent domain law in order to do a proper analysis of the property. To put it another way, there are plenty of appraisers that do bank appraisals. However, unless the bank appraiser has specifically done an eminent domain appraisal, and is familiar with severance damages, before and after valuation, offsite cures, and a host of other issues not found in a regular bank appraisal, then the bank appraiser is not qualified to do a proper valuation for an eminent domain taking.

You need an experienced eminent domain counsel, who has worked with experienced eminent domain experts to properly analyze, evaluate and value the property taken, and the impact the condemning authorities taking is having on any remaining property. Without having properly experienced expert witnesses, the property owner's appraisal could be attacked at trial and could be thrown out by the trial court. Therefore, it is very important that you have experienced eminent domain counsel to select the expert witnesses needed for the eminent domain case.

What is the Role of the Eminent Domain Attorney?

The easiest way to describe the eminent domain attorney is to compare him or her to the quarterback on a football team. He or she must coordinate and lead their team of experts in the case against the condemning authority's attorney and host of expert witnesses. Experienced eminent domain counsel is the backbone of your condemnation case. You should choose one who has sufficient eminent domain experience and a history of successfully representing property owners.

Like doctors, attorneys also specialize in fields of law. You would not see a foot doctor if you had a problem with your heart. That is the same for eminent domain counsel. You want someone who practices exclusively in eminent domain, as it is a highly specialized field.

Many eminent domain attorneys have been practicing this area of law for 10 to 20 years or more. Many, at some point in their career, have worked for condemning authorities, gaining valuable eminent domain experience.

The eminent domain attorney has a multi-faceted role in an eminent domain case. He or she will be the property owner's main contact person in the case. The eminent domain attorney must be able to explain the eminent domain process, the case and the law to the property or business owner, and let them know what to expect during the life of the case. Only through clear communications between the client and eminent domain counsel will the client be able to understand the various facets of the case, and be in the best position to decide what is best for his or her property or business.

Eminent domain counsel must do some preliminary investigation of the case and condemnation project to determine some of the issues that will need expert witness work. From this initial investigation, a good eminent domain attorney will choose the team of experts that is best suited for the case. The attorney will give the experts their working assignments and coordinate their efforts on the case. A good eminent domain attorney will call meetings of his or her expert witnesses so that all the issues are uncovered and discussed and everyone is working toward a common goal. A good eminent domain attorney will also engage in additional investigation of the case to uncover all the evidence that the condemning authority has on the case. A good eminent domain attorney will do this through public records requests for documents to the condemning authority and discovery requests. Public records requests can be made at any time, but are most effective prior to the condemnation case being filed. Discovery is simply the legal method of investigating the opposing party's case by requesting documents, and posing written questions that the opposing party must answer.

Once a condemnation suit is filed, the eminent domain attorney also will accept service of process; review all of the condemning authority's pleadings and discovery; file the appropriate answer and defenses in the case; attend and participate in the Order of Taking hearing; take the depositions of all of the condemning authority's witnesses; and conduct the trial of the case. Additionally, if the client is a business owner or tenant, the eminent domain attorney will hire the best forensic accountant, and any other witnesses needed to draft a business damage claim, and have the business damage claim filed within the statutory guidelines so the damages are preserved.

Eminent domain counsel will also participate in any negotiations or court ordered mediations, and will advise the client of all his options in both negotiations or a trial of the eminent domain matter. A good eminent domain attorney will guide the property owner, business owner or tenant through the entire condemnation process. He or she will ensure that the property owner, business owner or tenant is paid full and fair compensation for any property that is taken, paid any damages to any remaining property, and paid any damages to the business or leasehold.

Why do I Need an Eminent Domain Attorney?

First and foremost, the eminent domain process can be very long and complicated. There are a number of rules and time deadlines that apply in an eminent domain case. You need to not only be thoroughly familiar with the statutory law on eminent domain, but a person must also be intimately familiar with the thousands of eminent domain cases handed down by our appellate courts in the state of Florida, and how they apply to the present case. Oftentimes, these appellate cases interpret the statutory law and demonstrate the application between the case law and the facts in a given case. Additionally, knowledge of the Rules of Civil Procedure, Evidence Law, Constitutional Law, Administrative Law, City, County and Local Government Law, and a myriad of other legal areas are needed to properly defend an eminent domain case, and ensure that the property owner receives full compensation in the case.

Second, and just as important, the condemning authority will have legal counsel and expert witnesses at its ready disposal to help it get the lowest price possible for the land or business it is taking or damaging. In order to balance the playing field, the statutes and cases in Florida require that all attorney's fees and costs incurred by the property owner, business owner or tenant are paid for by the condemning authority at the end of the case. In other words, any property owner, business owner or tenant that is affected by an eminent domain matter is entitled to get his or her fees and costs paid in full. As eminent domain counsel, I rely on the statute for the payment of my attorney's fees and costs, and the fees and costs for my experts. The client in an eminent domain matter is billed nothing for the attorney's work on the case, or for the work of the expert witnesses. Therefore, by having legal counsel trained in eminent domain, with the ability to hire expert witnesses to counter the condemning authority's experts, the property owner, business owner and tenant are put on a level playing field with the power of the government. In this manner, the client is in the best position to receive full compensation for the property taken, damages to the remainder, and any business or leasehold damages that might have occurred due to the condemnation.

Third, there are changes to the eminent domain case law and statutes each year. A good eminent domain counsel keeps up with the latest changes and trends in the eminent domain field, and is in the best position to advise the client of how these changes might affect his or her property or business.

Fourth, when the property owner, business owner or tenant discusses the matter with the condemning authority, or one of its agents, the condemning authority can later use these conversations against the property owner, business owner or tenant in court, if the matter goes to trial. Conducting all matters associated with the condemnation through an eminent domain attorney prevents these conversations from being used against the client in court. For example, if the property owner were to tell the condemning authority he or she felt the property was worth X dollars, that statement could be used against the property owner in court, even if the property was actually worth many times more.

Fifth, an eminent domain attorney is specially trained to recognize legal and factual issues that can help a client receive full compensation. The eminent domain attorney knows what experts will be needed to prove fair market value, highest and best use, and get the client full compensation. The eminent domain attorney will review and analyze the condemning authority's offer to the client, and advise the client if the condemning authority's offer is acceptable or unacceptable and the reasons for that advice.

Sixth, the eminent domain attorney can review the government's public purpose, necessity and good faith offer, and can sometimes delay or permanently stop a taking at the Order of Taking hearing, if it is in the client's best interests. There are situations in an eminent domain case where the government's case does not meet the necessary prerequisites to acquire the property. In these instances, a delay in the case may be an advantage to the property owner, such as when the real estate market is appreciating. On the other hand, there may be situations where the government cannot correct a problem in their condemnation suit and the taking can be stopped permanently.

Seventh, the eminent domain attorney will conduct the trial on the matter and will cross-examine the government's witnesses. The attorney will put on the client's witnesses to prove the fair market value of the property, the severance damages, and the value of the business damages or leasehold interest -- among some of the areas where damages can be recovered in a condemnation case.

These seven reasons are just some of the areas demonstrating why eminent domain counsel is needed to guide the property owner, business owner or tenant through the complex process of eminent domain. Eminent domain counsel is there to answer the client's questions and ensure that the client receives full and fair compensation in the eminent domain case.

How do I Choose an
Eminent Domain Attorney?

Choosing an eminent domain attorney is an important process. Ultimately, you will need to be comfortable with the attorney you choose because you will be spending a lot of time with the attorney. As a client, you want to know that you can call the attorney any time you have a question. Two-way communication between the attorney and the client is essential in an eminent domain case.

You want an attorney who is experienced in eminent domain law. Most seasoned eminent domain attorneys have been doing eminent domain for more than 10 years. In Florida, unlike many other areas of the law, the number of eminent domain attorneys practicing this area of law is limited. Consequently, many seasoned eminent domain attorneys handle cases throughout the state.

You might want to consider if the eminent domain counsel you hire has ever worked for the condemning authority. This can be an important factor since it gives your eminent domain counsel inside knowledge of the workings of the condemning authority or governmental entity, and how it does its cases.

Determine if the eminent domain counsel you hire will charge you any upfront fees or costs. Some attorneys, especially ones that do not do a lot of eminent domain, might charge you upfront fees. I practice exclusively eminent domain and I rely entirely on the eminent domain statutes for my fees and costs. The client is never charged for any fees and costs in any eminent domain case I do.

Find out if your attorney is Board Certified by The Florida Bar. In Florida, an attorney cannot hold himself or herself out to be Board Certified unless he or she has practiced a minimum number of years in the area of law, has been reviewed and approved by a number of his or her peers in the area, and has passed a rigorous Board Certification Exam. Additionally, a Board Certified attorney must take continuing legal education in his or her area of certification, above and beyond the continuing legal education needed for the average attorney. Although an attorney does not need to be Board Certified to practice eminent domain law, certification demonstrates the attorney's continuing pursuit of legal and professional excellence.

You should never make a choice of your attorney based on advertising alone. You should take the time to investigate the background of the attorney you are about to hire, it will make the entire condemnation process much easier, and ask some of the following questions:

- How long has the attorney been in practice?
- How long has the attorney been practicing eminent domain?
- Does the attorney specialize in just eminent domain, or does he or she do other practice areas?
- Is the attorney knowledgeable about eminent domain law?
- Has the attorney ever taught eminent domain law at a law school?
- Does the attorney have an open door policy so you can call him or her to answer your questions, or discuss your case?
- Does the attorney's law firm have a good reputation?
- Is the attorney highly rated by Martindale-Hubbell or another bona fide rating agency?
- Is your attorney Board Certified by The Florida Bar?
- Has the attorney ever been disciplined by The Florida Bar?

Will I owe Money for Attorney's Fees, Costs or Expert Fees?

No, you will not owe any money for attorney's fees, costs, or expert fees or costs in an eminent domain case. The statutes in the state of Florida require that a property owner, business owner, or tenant shall have all his attorney's fees and costs, and expert fees and costs, paid by the condemning authority. An attorney should not require the payment of an attorney's fee or costs to represent you in an eminent domain matter. Almost all attorneys practicing eminent domain in the state of Florida will rely on the statute for payment of attorney's fees and costs, and expert fees and costs. If you have an attorney who wants to charge you for doing your eminent domain case, you should consider calling other eminent domain attorneys.

Attorney's fees in eminent domain are paid differently than in other cases. The condemning authority is required by statute to pay the attorney's fees and costs in an eminent domain matter. The attorney's fees are paid over and above the amount the property owner, business owner or tenant is awarded at trial or through negotiated settlement. None of the attorney's fees and costs come out of the award to the client. Only in this manner is the client made whole for the taking of his property. As an example, the client is offered $50,000 by the condemning authority for his property. At mediation or trial, the client is awarded $100,000. The client keeps the entire $100,000 and the attorney is paid his fees and costs by the condemning authority in a separate hearing.

What are the Tax Consequences in Eminent Domain Proceedings?

The following is not tax advice and should not be construed as such. It is simply information for your consideration.

You should always consult your tax advisor as to the tax consequences in an eminent domain action. Each individual's tax issues can be different. However, the transfer of property to a condemning authority in an eminent domain proceeding constitutes an exchange for tax purposes and is a taxable event to the owner of the property.

If the owner of business or investment property realizes a loss on the disposition, the loss must be recognized immediately, because nothing in the Internal Revenue Code prohibits the tax recognition of the loss simply because the sale was an involuntary one. Section 1033 of the IRS Code provides an alternative to the otherwise mandatory, immediate recognition of the gain. In these instances, the owner generally may defer recognition of the gain to the extent he or she continues the original investment by reinvesting the condemnation proceeds in property similar to that seized by the condemning authority. The taxpayer recognizes gain in qualifying transactions only to the extent that the amount realized on the conversion exceeds the cost of the qualifying replacement property. To the extent all the condemnation proceeds are reinvested in qualifying property, any resulting gain can be deferred for tax purposes in exchange for a reduction in the tax basis of the replacement property.